WHEN I WAS A BOY

MEMOIRS OF AN AGING PREACHER

George's Journey

GEORGE PASS SR.

BookVenture Publishing LLC
1000 Country Lane Ste 300
Ishpeming MI 49849
www.bookventure.com
Hotline: 1(877) 276-9751
Fax: 1(877) 864-1686

Ordering Information:
Quantity sales. Special discounts are available on quantity purchases by corporations, associations, and others. For details, contact the publisher at the address above.

Printed in the United States of America.

Library of Congress Control Number		2019940023
ISBN-13:	Softcover	978-1-64557-110-0
	Hardcover	978-1-64557-109-4
	Pdf	978-1-64557-111-7
	ePub	978-1-64557-112-4
	Kindle	978-1-64557-113-1

Rev. date: 04/17/2019

Contents

A Tribute to My Wife, Janet P. Pass

She was there with all our five children!

She was there when I accepted the call into the *ministry*!

She was there when I was sent to my first church assignment!

She was there when the ministry had a sale, and *she* cooked all the chicken!

She was there at our first communion, and she baked the communion bread!

She was there at every renovation and building experience of our first church to encourage me!

She was there and helped organize my doctoral ceremony and celebration!

She was there when I was sent to pastor, and we changed the name of the church to the Garden of Eden COGIC!

She was there when I rebuilt the church from the ground up in Eden, North Carolina!

She was there when I transferred into the Second Episcopal District of the AME Church!

She was there at every pastoral appointment (6)!

She was there at every sickness, affliction, and injuries that happened!

I shall retire from the African Methodist Episcopal Church in 2019.

She was there!

Acknowledgement

I want to tell everyone just how much I appreciate your interest in this book. In a very real way these writings shows how God has taken my life and prepared me for his will and purpose. While it reveals a lot of my personal experiences, I'm hoping that the things I've gone through will serve as an encouragement as well an enlightenment for the readers. To show us that in spite of the way our life turns, God is still in control. I think perhaps all of us has a story to tell. For me there are some that really stands out that shows the stamina, the breaking, and the healing that comes from one who has depended on the Lord's power and strengths to get through all that life has handed me. I know without a doubt that I could not have gone through these experiences alone.

My mother, Myrtle Evelyn Penn Pass, was such a pillar and strong force who taught me how to hang in there and presented the God who I serve to this day. My wife, Janet Person Pass, who stood with me throughout our fifty-four years of marriage, when things were good, when things were not so good, and when things were in turmoil. I thank her for her love for me and for her forgiveness during those difficult days. I want to thank all my children, Rev. Sonji Y. Pass, Bishop George A. Pass II, Mr. Scott A. Pass Sr., the late Bishop Jeffrey R. Pass, and Ms. Jerri L. Pass Price, who in their own way loved me even when it was a challenge for them. They each contributed to the success of my being a father, and I thank them for the support each gave to me. To all my friends and associates who down through the years have contributed to my development in every stage of my life. My pastor Bishop Wyoming W. Wells, who poured into my life both as a man and as a preacher. He richly influenced my life in a very special way. My brothers and sister who were always candid with me, from the oldest brother Orville V. Pass, James (Bobby) Jamal Robert

Pass, Ruth Elaine (Lefleur, Oliver) Pass, and, of course, Samuel Penn Pass. And to all my relatives who in their own way helped me in one way or another. Many thanks to Toni Shaw's Photography for doing an excellent job with my photo shoot and making me picturesque.

I certainly want to give my appreciation to Sherry who took the time out of her busy schedule to read and sketch the illustrations for each of my stories.

I really thank all of you for what you've done to me and what you've done for me. May the blessing of the Lord be upon each of you.

My First Jump

I was the youngest of three boys at that time. Ruth and Sammy hasn't been born yet. My brothers took up a whole lot of time with me. I was exposed to many of the things that they were caught up in, like rolling car tires in the neighborhood. I was so small that they could put me inside the tire—that is, putting my feet at the bottom of the tire and my head on top of the tire. Then they would roll me around the area where we lived. I don't know who came up with that idea, but I loved my brothers and would do whatever they ask of me.

One day my brothers were rolling me around and got to a slight hill. The tire was rolling faster than they could keep up with it, and it got away from both of them. There I was rolling down the street, getting farther and farther away from them. They were terrified because they lost control of the situation. They began hollering, fearful of what could happen to me. As for me, I thought it was fun rolling down the street at such a fast pace. After what seemed like a long ride, the tire finally came to a stop and fell over on its side. When they finally caught up to me, they were really relieved to see that I wasn't hurt in any way, maybe a little dizzy. We all laughed about it, and they made me promise not to tell Mah (our mother). I guess that experience taught me to be tough and how to keep a secret. We had many more experiences together as siblings.

There was one other time when the boys in the neighborhood would get together and play parachuting. You see Mr. Anderson had a garage at the back of his house, which was like an alley on the side of our house. The garage was low in the back and went up to about twelve feet in the front. You see, we could go around to the back of his garage, climb up on it, and go up to the front at the highest point, and then jump off and land on our feet. We called that parachuting in the air. I would watch the other kids, along with my brothers, jumping off that garage and going around the back, climbing up again, jumping off over and over again. Well, while I was the youngest and the smallest, something in me wanted to do it too. It looked like so much fun until I got my chance to climb up on the back of the garage and had a hard time getting up on it. I was maybe two or three years old at the time. When I got to the front of the garage, it almost scared me to death. You see at that time I have never been that high in my life. I remember standing on top of that garage at the very edge looking down at the ground and thinking I could die or break something! But everybody was encouraging and cheering me on. After what seemed like an hour, although it wasn't really that long, I got up enough nerve to jump off. I did jump even when I was really scared. I remember landing on my feet, and my knees hit me in my chest so hard it almost took my breath away. It really hurt for a while, but something in me drove me to do it again, and again, and again. I was parachuting too along with the other guys there. I guess I learned from that experience to overcome fear and not to be afraid to conquer whatever is facing me at the time!

A Short Story

I was around eight years old when we—that is, some of my friends at the time—would go on what we call an expedition. On this particular day, which was a Sunday, after Sunday school, my mother allowed me to leave and not stay for the morning service. We went for a long walk and ended up at A & T's farm. Well, on that farm, not far from where they kept the bull, was a pond. This pond had a barge on it, and guess what we decided to do? You got it, we climbed on that barge, not thinking of the end results. Some of us had our Sunday suits on, which was wool, and others had casual clothes on. But we went on out there. Now the pond was of some size, big enough for us to play on it for hours if we chose to. There was also a pole that was about twenty feet long to push yourself along on the barge. Well, we had no idea that the pond was deep until we found out that it was deeper than the pole. *Oh man*, we thought and then started to panic. Somebody said, "I'm hitting the water." When we couldn't touch the bottom of the pond with the pole, we just let it go in the water and everybody jumped in the water and began swimming back to the edges of the pond, suit and shoes and everything that we had on. One of A&T's workers saw us and began running toward us, hollering and yelling at us, which made us more excited as he ran after us. We got out of the water and ran and jumped the fence again. We were miles from where we lived, and in August the days would still get pretty hot. Well, me and my wet wool suit walked home the long way just in case someone tried to follow us. My wool suit began to dry out and started drawing up. And the drier it got, the more it drew up. By the time we got home I looked like I had long shorts on, and the coat I just took it off. After I got back home, I took off the suit and hid it so my mother wouldn't see it and punish me for what I had done.

That experience taught me that "without trusting God, you might be up the creek without a paddle."

If we had waited and not panicked, the barge would have drifted over to the edge of the pond on its own and there would have been a better outcome for us.

Mysterious Blackbird

I'm trying to understand this even at my age now. When I was a boy, I saw this big blackbird just sitting on the ground in the parking lot of the Paradise Drive-In and I walked right up to it. I picked it up thinking something must be wrong with it. I cradled it in my bosom and carried the bird home with me so I could nurse it back to health. Well, I fed it water and simply stroked it and let it rest all that afternoon. When my mother came home from work, for she never knew what I would have there, she told me that I had better get that bird out of her house. So that evening before dark, I took the bird outside and threw her in the air. She simply flew away, never looking back. To this day I never knew what that meant, if anything at all—that is, until recently my wife saw another bird lying on our front porch. The bird looked as if it flew into the wall and fell dead. After carefully examining the poor little creature, we could say that it was barely alive. Being so concerned about that little bird, I sat a small container of water at it. I tried to feed some of the water by putting its little beak in the water, not sure if it was receiving anything. Well, we covered the little fellow with a small crate to protect it from any prey that might be in the neighborhood. We checked on the bird often during the day to see how it was progressing. Each time we checked the little bird it was moving around more and more. That went on for about three days, and on third day, when we checked, the bird had flown away. I'm yet again puzzled about my contact with these little creatures of God!

I Lost My Youngest Brother
When He Was Two Years Old!

I am seven years older than my younger brother. I was such a carefree fellow, inquisitive about most of everything. I could lose myself in my thoughts or, at best, imagination.

My mother worked first and sometimes second shifts at L. Richardson Hospital. On this particular day she told me to watch my little brother Sammy and not let anything happen to him. I'm thinking, *I'm just nine years old and have to go on expeditions every day.* I learned to take care of my chores and activities that were given to me, but sometimes I forgot and would be gone from the house. I watched him for as long as I could stand it, but soon felt my journey calling me. I left.

I wasn't gone that long, maybe two or three hours the most, when I started thinking, *It's almost time for Mother to get off work and where is my little brother Sammy?*

I started making my way back home to make sure everything that I was supposed to do was in order. When I got home, Sammy was nowhere to be found. I started calling and searching for him. First in the house, and when he wasn't there, I started getting nervous. Where in the world could that boy be? I started going to different houses around the neighborhood to see if he was there, and when he wasn't there, I really started to panic. My mother would be home in a little bit, and my worst thought was that she was going to kill me because I've lost my little brother. I couldn't come back home until I find him.

I started running from door to door, hollering and yelling, "Sammy!" I was scared almost to death while thinking the worst. My thoughts got worse. My fear of the worst thing happening got worse. I was scared to death to go home by now because my little brother was somewhere dead! I stayed out until about ten o'clock that night in tortured fear of what my mother is going through because of her baby and of what she is going to do to me because of what happened to her baby.

My imagination had gone beyond its sober rationality. I'm about to die, y'all. I slowly started toward the house and thinking the worst with every step. I finally got to the house. I had to tell my mother that I don't know where Sammy is. I just know she was going to kill me, I mean, literally. I was scared to death! When I got in the house getting ready for my death sentence, I heard my little brother in the living room talking to my mother. Needless to say, my heart was overwhelmed and overjoyed at the same time. My little brother was home. I never told my mother, and she never let on that she knew what had happened. I guess she figured it was enough suffering and whipping for me.

He Took My Christmas Tree

The Grove, which was short for Lincoln Grove, was a neighborhood on the east side of Greensboro. In those days it was a close-knit area with good family values and pride, and it was full of woods. It was a tremendous play area for a lot of us kids. It would be very common for us to use our imagination like riding down small trees as bucking wild horses. The trees would sometimes reach heights of thirty to forty feet. We would climb to the top of the trees and sway from side to side until the weight of our bodies would ride the tree to the ground. Then we would start jumping up and down on the tree limb. Best bucking rodeo any boy could experience.

Well, we were deep in the woods and the thought of finding a Christmas tree came to my mind since it was getting close to Christmas. I and another friend were together playing while looking for a tree. We came across the prettiest small Christmas tree that you'd ever see. I guess it stood about four feet tall. It was taller than me and my friend. We took our knives and scored around the base of tree and broke it off. Most every little boy in our neighborhood that time had a small pocket knife. It was going to make my mother so proud of me for finding such a gorgeous Christmas tree. It was my tree since I saw it first; my friend just helped me. Man, we were so excited about the tree, just laughing and jumping as we dragged the tree through the woods.

Both me and my friend were small for our ages and never expected of what seemed like a giant of a guy coming through the woods meeting us as we were walking. When he saw the tree and how small we were, he knew we could never be a competition to him. He bullied us and took my Christmas tree. I was wounded in my heart and felt so violated as I watched the man take my Christmas tree out of sight. I just stood there for I don't know how long, dealing with the feelings that I couldn't describe at the time. I did say when I got big enough I was going to get that guy, but as time went on, I couldn't remember what he even looked like. I do remember spending a little more time in the woods looking for another Christmas tree, but I never saw another one.

You never know what experiences in life that are designed to make you strong enough to take care of yourself.

The Songs Made Me Feel Strange

Living in the projects afforded us exposure to various social groups and ministries that would come and share their gifts and talents with us especially during the summer months.

I remember these missionaries that would come to the office and set up chairs and a small table up in the front, and each one of them would take turns coming in front of us kids. One of them would teach us songs like "Heavenly Sunshine," "This Little Light of Mine," "My Cup Is Full and Running Over," and "Down in My Heart Today."

There was something about these songs that made me feel real strange. I couldn't explain it, but I know that I like them and they were very moving for me. It seemed that the more we sang them, the more I wanted to sing them. There was something else too. One of them told a story about a prophet who went to a widow's house. The people that time were very hungry and starving. The woman, who had only one son, was going to fix her last meal, then she and her son was going to die. But the prophet told her to fix him a cake first and she will not run out of oil and flour.

I was speechless when the woman teaching the lesson poured what looked like oil out of a pitcher and every time she turned the pitcher up to pour, oil came out of it. She continued to turn that pitcher up, and oil came out of the pitcher every time. I was so overwhelmed. I couldn't hardly believe what I was seeing. It was more than magic; it was like a miracle. All that experience affected me more than I could even express. I didn't realize it, but it was one of the first stages in preparing me for ministry.

I Almost Drowned at the "Y"

I was a very daring kid as there wasn't much that I wouldn't try or even do. There were three or four places around that kept me out of trouble, which was pretty hard to do: The Center, where we went swimming, played basketball, and watch movies and played different games;

Carnegie Library, which was at that time the only black library in the area; the Palace Theater, which was the only black movie theater for us (We could pay one price and stay all day watching the same movies); and the Hayes Taylor YMCA. There you could get involved with many activities including swimming. They had what I thought was an official-size swimming pool, and so many of us wanted to go and swim in the pool.

Well, I could swim but I didn't learn to breathe the correct way. Anyway, I decided I was going to swim across the pool without stopping. I dived into the pool full of strength and excitement. I started stroking, getting my stride. I really felt real good starting out, but as I got closer to the other side, I started getting out of breath and energy. Well, I got to the place where I had to breathe, but I had not gotten to the other side yet. I remember thinking, *I have got to take a breath.* But I would have to take a mouthful of water. I was getting scared because that could be the end of me. Just as I was getting ready to breathe, *something or someone pushed me over to the edge of the pool*! When I touched the edge of the pool, I turned to see who helped me but there was no one within twenty feet of me. I tried telling my friends what happened, but they didn't believe me. It finally became all right with me whether they believed me or not. I figured later that it had to be an angel who saved me. From that point on in my life I started thinking that there was something different about me.

Let Me Try It

I have always been a curious person. I was in the seventh grade at Lincoln Junior High School, and we had just finished eating at lunchtime. Usually, we have about thirty minutes downtime for playing or simply relaxing before starting our afternoon classes. Well, I had just gone outside when I saw a few of my friends playing. I didn't really get the gist of what they were doing until I got closer to them. I saw that they were trying a wrestling move that was not really working for them. They were supposed to have the opponent take a deep breath and hold it. The opposing person was supposed to hold them around the chest from the back, and they were supposed to faint or fall out. I understand they were trying it on each other, but it was not working for any of them.

So I said, "*Let me try it.*"

Tommy White said, "Okay."

Well, he took a deep breath and held it. Standing behind him, I grabbed him from around his chest and squeezed him real tight. I had no idea of what I was doing as I held him for what seemed like a long time. However, it was about only a minute.

All of a sudden I heard a very loud holler, so I let Tommy go and he fell flat on his face. Oh! I looked at him, and he was out like a light. I thought he was dead. I thought I would wet myself out of fear. I was scared almost to death. In a little while he started coming around. We helped him up on his feet, and he asked what happened. I couldn't say or do anything for a while. Those that were there started talking about me, saying things like "Don't mess with George or he'll put that move on you." They were actually afraid of me, but little did they know that I had no idea what I was doing. I found out that I had to be very careful about saying, "*Let me try it,*" because things could happen! I can't tell you about the heavy-duty equipment tractors that none of my friends could start, but I said, "*Let me try it*!" But that's another story. Ha, ha, ha, ha!

Blackberries

I love blackberries, and as a boy I found a place that had the largest and prettiest blackberries around. They were so pretty, the neighborhood people were so impressed about it, not only the way they looked but its taste as well. They had such a sweet taste and aroma to them. I didn't realize it, but I seemed to have had a kind of get up and go about me, and sometimes it would get me involved in things that might be too challenging. A lot of times it would break my spirit or someone would not follow through to encourage me.

One day a man from our neighborhood saw the blackberries that we—that is, me and a few of my friends—had picked at that time. The man asked if we could get some more of those berries, and he would buy them from me.

I told him, "Yes, we could."

He told me that he would buy as many as I could get for him and that he would give me $2.00 a quart for them. I became so excited because I knew that with me and my two friends we could accomplish the challenge. So I told him we would, and he said okay!

Well, I had already figured that if we picked a pot full—that is, my mother's canning pot— that would be twenty quarts of blackberries. At $2.00 a quart, that would be $40.00. My head started spinning with an exciting throb in thinking I would give my friends $10.00

each and the rest would be mine. Wow, I couldn't hardly sleep that night just thinking of the money we were going to make from *just picking blackberries*! I told my two friends how we could make some money by picking the blackberries and that they would make $10.00 each. Hallelujah!

We rose up early the next morning at about six o'clock and met each other. Then we went to the field and started picking. We each had about a gallon container, for I had figured that it wouldn't take too very long filling the containers, emptying them, and then going back for more. It was amazing to each of us that every time we went to pick the blackberries, it was just as many there each time.

Well, after about three times, the twenty-gallon pot was filled and we were ready to make our delivery. Nobody had ever told me how to treat blackberries, or as far as that is concerned, any kind of fruit for that matter. All I knew is that whenever I saw fruits or berries in the grocery stores, they looked clean as if they had been washed. *Sssooo,* I rinsed the blackberries in water. I didn't know that the berries would start to get mushy as the day heated up.

So in excitement we walked to the man's house, which was a little better than a mile away, with the blackberries. We didn't take into consideration how far a mile was when you're walking. We didn't take into consideration how heavy the wet blackberries were over time. We didn't realize the heat would cause our berries to start a kind of fermentation process.

Well, when we got to Mr. Fulton's house (to protect the real person, this is not the real name), I knock on his door. I was so excited I almost couldn't stand it. He came to the door and really looked surprised to see me, like he didn't believe I would do it. He immediately started making excuses for us being there especially on a weekday. He finally acted like he was mad at us for bringing all those blackberries to his house. Remember now he told me that he would take all the blackberries that we picked. I later figured out that he didn't have the money to pay me for the blackberries. Then he scolded us for rinsing the blackberries, claiming we had ruined them and that they were not any good now. He blatantly told me that he is not taking these blackberries. There is no way that I can express or explain how heart-wrenching he made feel. I couldn't believe a grown man would treat a child the way he treated us. The hurt, the disappointment, the shock, the anger that I felt. I trusted him, and he did this to us outrightly without any kind of remorse. He shut the door on us and left us just standing there. I was speechless.

So we left carrying those blackberries with us. Needless to say, they were twice as heavy by now because we had to carry them back to where we started. It took a little while before we said anything to each other, and when we did, we called that man every name we could without saying bad words or cursing. As mad as we were, we just started smearing blackberries everywhere we stopped to take a break, starting with Mr. Fulton's driveway. We had to go through Dudley High School campus; and everywhere we saw, a bench or a table, we smeared blackberries. We finally dumped the rest of the blackberries on the last bench and table at the campus. After we damaged the property, we became very afraid of what we have done. We hoped no one saw what we did to the properties with the blackberries. I don't know about my other two friends, for we never talked about it again. But as for me, it became very hard for me to simply believe or even trust what an adult would say to me. I don't know when I outgrew that experience, but I would not want any child, or even an adult for that matter, to have the experience like we did. As we grew older, we didn't forget Mr. Fulton but it didn't discouraged or stop me from picking blackberries.

My Professional Singing Days

I was nineteen years old when I received the opportunity to sing with Jimmy Jones and the Sensationals.

Jimmy Jones was supposed to have been the world's greatest base singer at that time. He started out with the Richmond Harmonizers, which became the Harmonizing Four out of Richmond, Virginia. They were a professional quartet singing group. Jimmy Jones was known for his range in singing for he could sing so low until you could feel vibrations around you from his voice and then go into a hard high gospel range that would mesmerize you. I was already singing with a semiprofessional group called the Spiritual Wonders, a local quartet group in Greensboro, North Carolina. I didn't meet Jimmy until our first singing concert down east toward the coast. We started practicing weeks before the concert. I was already accustomed to rehearsals, for the Spiritual Wonders rehearsed twice a week throughout our existence. Our motto was "Practice makes perfect." If you were going to be very good, then you had to rehearse. So we took that part very seriously. There were three of us that went with Jimmy Jones from our local group: Joe McClain, who sang high tenor; James Kelly, who sang tenor; and, of course, me. I sang baritone. Together we had perfect harmony, and not bragging, but we were exceptionally good. We agreed with each other that we would go together, and if necessary, we would leave together.

My experience on the road, as they called it, was enjoyable and challenging to say the least. All the time we spent on the road was somewhat bittersweet for me. Sweet in that there was nothing like singing in different churches and auditoriums and seeing other people's reactions and response to the way you are singing. It was simply amazing to me to have such an experience. It was very much like therapy, I think, for people in the black community that were limited financially and in other areas in life. There weren't many places we could go outside of our own communities, and God knows monies were limited, and even decent jobs were limited. But we found a way to entertain ourselves and be entertained.

We lived up to the misunderstanding and misnomers about singers on the road—that is, that the average singer, especially male singers, had a girl in every town and that they were womanizers. I must explain to each of you that it might have been true for some but for the better part it's not true! Back in the days of our travels, we were faced with extreme prejudices and segregation, and because of that we couldn't go to some public places like hotels and restaurants. If we found a place to eat, many times it was in the back of a white restaurant or a café up some alley that was not safe and was filthy. You really didn't know what you were getting when you order food or what was its condition. I suppose some of you have heard of the Green Book. It was a directory for blacks; and it give the names of hotels and restaurants across the country, and a few international places as well, that one could go and stay. But everybody couldn't afford many of those places.

There were names of boarding houses, rooming houses, and low-end nightspots where you could stay without sleeping in your car or wherever you were traveling in that were passed down by word of mouth. Because of that, many of the females felt sorry for us and would take us home with them. We were assured of a safe place to stay and a good hot meal. Some of the other women would see that and become jealous of the situation and would start spreading rumors about the singers. Some of it was true, but a lot of it was false. We really sang on the road for the love of singing because there wasn't much money in it, being that in many places the tickets were only one dollar. Of course, some groups did much better than others, especially if you were the more popular group. I was introduced to many of my fellow artists, women too. The Mighty Clouds of Joy, even at that time, was the most favorite group on the road. There others like The Gospel Consulators, Madame Edna Galmon Cook, the Soul Stirrers, the Davis Sisters, The Bind Boys from Mississippi and Alabama, Bro Joe Mays, and

The Gospelaires were just a few of the groups I traveled and sang with during those days

The experience on the road also boosted my confidence as a singer and performer in front of an audience. I know it helped me get to know the audience, to recognize their body language. It also made me more aware of my need of a savior too, for most of us were much lacking in that area. I remember after coming off the road that I hooked back up with the Spiritual Wonders again. We were in Wilmington, North Carolina, singing in a morning service at one church, an afternoon concert at an auditorium, and, of course, that night we are to sing at another church as well. I had already told the fellows that when we finished that weekend, I wouldn't be coming back home with them. I had planned to go up the coast and look for a job, and wherever my hat fell, that's where I would stay. I already knew Janet Person, who is my wife now, but back then we were just friends. We would talk on and off. She had very strong conviction of her love for Jesus Christ. In other words, she was saved.

Well, the fellows told her of my plans without my knowing it. She was a singer in her own right and asked our manager if she could come with us to the singing programs in Wilmington. We always had a place to rest and relax at Rev. Earl Cheek's house, and he said yes. I wondered what she was doing here, but I didn't say anything, and she didn't say anything until the Monday after the weekend concerts. She told me that she wanted to talk to me, and I gave her a chance to talk. She started telling me that she heard of my plans to leave the group and start up the coast to look for a job. She was telling me that she didn't think that was what I was supposed to do, but if I came back to Greensboro and gave the Lord my heart, He would work miracles and work everything out for me. I don't know why I was even listening to her, but I believed her and took her at her word. I came back to Greensboro and found out that there was a revival at the church that I used to belong to. When I went to that revival the following week, it seemed the message being preached was directed toward me. When the call to discipleship was made, I went to the altar and surrendered my life to the Lord. The very next week I found a job, and everything seemed to fall into place. Well, I want you to know that eventually I married that girl and I am still married to her till this day. That's been well over fifty years. Thank God!

God's Calling to Me

I was married in August 1964, and around October of that same year Janet and I joined Wells Temple COGIC in Greensboro, North Carolina, where Bishop Wyoming Wells was pastor. We started having a family in 1965 with our first daughter, Sonji Yvette Pass. She was the prettiest little girl anybody could ever see. Toward the end of 1966 I started feeling like the Lord was calling me to preach. I can hardly describe how that feels. Well, it was like a deep-down burning that didn't hurt, but it was very intense, like an itch that you couldn't scratch. Finally, I told my pastor, Bishop Wyoming Wells, how I was feeling. To my surprise he told me to go back and pray for two more weeks and if I felt the same way after that, then to let him know and maybe he would talk to me about it. Needless to say, I was very hurt and was thinking he didn't want to acknowledge it or maybe didn't want anything to do with me preaching.

After the two weeks were completed, I didn't get to say anything to him. He approached me, and of course, I told him that I felt the same way. He set up a time for me to meet with him, and the day came when I met him at his office. Upon entering his office, it felt as if I was going into a sanctuary of sorts. He came in and sat down behind what seemed like a very large desk. It looked like he was sitting on some kind of throne for he was six feet five inches tall and weighed about three hundred pounds. I really didn't know how to feel, but I know it was a very serious moment. He began the conversation by asking me why I felt like the Lord was calling me to preach.

I started explaining to him how every night for about a week I would awaken somewhere around 2:00 a.m. The first two nights I wondered why I would wake up knowing that I had to go to work in the morning. On the second night it dawned on me that maybe I need to pray, so I did. I fell asleep while I was on my knees. The third night I awakened at around the same time, and in my prayers, I remember asking the Lord was there something wrong with me. That was when the Lord said to me, "*I want you to preach my word.*" The voice wasn't audible, but it was so intense, I knew it was Him. I began to make excuses as to why I couldn't do it, like "Lord, I can't do that because I don't know any scriptures." He would counter my excuses with scripture, like "*I qualify whom I calleth.*" I didn't know it was scripture until later on. I told the Lord, "Won't nobody believe me with the way I had lived?" He said to me, "*You go and I'll go with you and will speak for you.*" Little did I know that was scripture also. I had been going to Sunday school and Bible study, but I still didn't think I knew enough to preach. But the Lord reminded me of the experience of Moses in the Bible, when God talked to him in the burning bush. He told Moses to put his hand into his bosom, and when he took it out, his hand was white with leprosy. Then he told Moses to put his hand back into his bosom, and when he took it out, his hand was back to normal. I was simply overwhelmed at what the Lord was saying to me. Finally, toward the end of the week, *I said yes to the Lord!*

Bishop Wells just looked at me with a pleasant look and a calmness about himself and with a look of approval. Then he started talking to me and said, *"Georgie boy, I can't promise you that I will make you a good preacher. That will have to be up to you, but I will promise you this—if you listen to me, I will make a man out of you!"* He told me that when he makes the announcement of me becoming a preacher, I will never be able to take it back. I would be a preacher for the rest of my life. While my friends and classmates start to retire, I won't be able too. He went on to say many things to me about staying in prayer and studying the word of God to become sound in it. He talked about the different books I needed that would help me in scripture understanding. There were three major books I needed to read first apart from a good Bible. He mentioned the Scofield Bible, *Mathew Henry's Interpretations of the Bible*, and *Cruden's Concordance of the Bible*. He went on to teach me about preaching and what not to do about preaching. He did tell me this: "*When you get up to preach, start slow, rise high, strike fire, and then sit down!*" If you start preaching and the people say "Amen," then say it again. If you are preaching, and the congregation gets up and starts shouting and praising the Lord, then there is no need to try to keep preaching. He said, "*Shut up and start praising the Lord with them. There's no need to say anything else!*" Read everything that you can, even the billboards on the highway, and you will never run out of something to say. And pray more than you read. I guess he told me about prayer because praying keeps you humble and focused, to keep you from getting off and becoming a heretic!

Well, he called Mother Wells into the office and told her of the good news about me accepting the call of God in my life. She simply started to rejoice and be glad for me. She said that she would do everything she could to encourage me. I was looking so solemn until she said to me, "Elder George, stop looking so sad and be glad." I took her advice. One of the most important things to me in all this is the relationship I had with Bishop Wells and how he taught me how to be a man of God! Not only that but also how to be a husband to my wife and a father to my children. Having the church as a covering has disciplined me in preparing for the ministering of the Lord's gospel. Hallelujah!

The Beginning!

We were just finishing our morning worship at Wells Temple Church of God in Christ on the fourteenth of December 1969. I was carrying some of Bishop Well's things back to the office when Mother Wells met me in the hall and asked if I was going to Winston-Salem with the church, for the announcement was made during the service that the bishop was going to dedicate the opening of a new ministry. I told her that I didn't plan to go, but since she asked, then I would.

The church was in Winston-Salem and was a small storefront building way at the back side of a dead-end road that look like it would only seat about seventy-five people, if that many. The little pulpit was just big enough to seat Bishop Wells, Elder James Gales, Elder Jonathan Cureton, and myself; and we're sitting on top of each other then. After Bishop Wells preached and did the dedication toward the close of the service, he announced who he felt like the Lord was telling him to leave there as the pastor. I had no idea that he was going to appoint a preacher there at that time. He said that after praying, the Lord revealed to him who it was. He said to the Lord, "Are you sure, Lord?" And the Lord said yes!

I was really expecting Bishop Wells to call one of the other ministers who were there. *When he called my name*, I was so surprised and shocked that I became weak all over and almost fell out of the chair. I had no idea what to do from that point on. I was so shocked as I least expected that kind of announcement. So after the service, I asked the bishop what was I supposed to do. His reply was, "Son, go pastor your church." Little did I know that my life will never be the same.

I told the ones that were there that I would see them on Tuesday night for Bible study. It was customary in those days that Tuesday nights were Bible study nights and Friday nights were Pastor's Aide Night. While the little place was packed that Sunday, when I got there that

Tuesday, there were only seven people: Deacon James and Missionary Lillian Johnson; Miss Mary Jackson; and three of her daughters, Joan, Elaine (Fruitee), and Robin. Of course, there was a cousin, Denise (Neesy) Blackwell.

We continued to have service in the little storefront building for some time after that, but I felt like we could do better. So the Johnsons found another place closer to town on Nothwest Boulevard. It was a little larger than the other place and on Main Street as well. As we continued our services, we had people come in off the street, adults and children as well. They eventually joined the church, of course. There were family members, brothers, sisters, cousins, and some other friends. I was very thankful that the Lord was adding to the mission church. We started organizing and developed a Sunday school department and a youth choir. I had no idea that our children could really sing, which really helped the church because people loved to hear good singing.

I was somewhat surprised when the enemy started to stir things up as the Johnsons were trying to start another church and take all the members with them without my knowing, but God has a way that is beyond your not knowing about a thing, even your own ignorance. Once I found out I confronted them about it, and it was true. They told me that they would not and could not have anything to do with Love Grove COGIC. It wasn't long before the Johnsons left and started another ministry outside of Winston-Salem.

In the meantime my wife had had our last child, and she was able to join me in the ministry. We then moved to a church building right around the corner from where we were. The Johnsons had already started to miss services, and in one of our services, an older lady came in the church and said she was looking for a church home, and when she heard the singing and praising God, she knew that was the place for it. Mother Louise Crompton was the first older person who joined our church, so I started calling her Mother Crompton. Well, the old lady who owned the church building saw how the Lord was prospering our services and blessing our church. She called and told me that the members could stay there but I had to leave. I really think she wanted to keep the people who were there and be in charge of them herself, not realizing that people are attracted to the ministry and not just the person. With me not having much church experience, I told my pastor, Bishop Wells, about the situation. He said that he would talk to see if he could work things out. So I gave him her number, and he called her. When she found out he was calling on my behalf, she went off on him and would not let him say anything. So he just politely hung up the phone and told me to go get my people and find another place to worship.

My wife Jan has always had an excellent eye for finding places, and she saw a building up on corner of Twenty-Fifth Street and Manchester. It was a two-story rooming house with two commercial businesses in the front. It also had a basement that had never been used for anything. Well, I called the owner of the building, and he told me that it had never been used for anything but if we cleaned out, we could start holding services there and he wouldn't charge us anything for using it. We were so excited to have finally found a place that all of us chipped in and started cleaning it out. It was so filthy that we began to get sores on our noses and had to find masks to wear so we wouldn't get sick from the skeletal pest and rodents and the filth from the place. *But we got through it with the Lord's help*! We painted the floors and built an altar and pulpit. We even had a kneeling place around the altar. We had some wonderful services there, and the Lord really added to our church. One of my sons, George II, who had been playing piano since about four years old, began to play the organ for the church. He was so short his feet couldn't barely touch the pedals. The place had two parts, so we had our sanctuary on one side and fellowship area with offices on the other. Some people donated pews that were the right size. Someone even donated a used forced-air furnace that we installed. It seemed to be the perfect place, but the ceiling was just so low.

Bishop Wells came to encourage us, and some members from Wells Temple COGIC in Greensboro, North Carolina, also came with him. Bishop Wells was so tall, he couldn't raise his hands up. He had to stretch them out. That was funny to see. We got a big laugh out of that. The service was exceptional with the praising of God and the preaching of the Word.

The church on Manchester served as a growing spurt for us and was doing better spiritually and physically. I started to think about a permanent place of worship for our congregation. With that being said, I was riding up Liberty St. one day and noticed a two-story house for sale and for some reason I could visualize a church in that house. I went in and talked with the owner about what I had in mind, and he did an owner financing with me. The property also had a small commercial building attached to it, and I also envisioned having services in that small building while I renovated the house into a chapel of about 150 people.

We—that is, the members and I—began preparing the building for service as I began planning for the two-story house to be converted into a church for the Lord. The men started helping me demolish the old roof and cut away the second story of the house. There was a large fireplace right at the center of the house. That also had to be taken out brick by brick. After some time the excavation was finally done but not without people potentially falling off the building and possibly getting hurt or maybe killed. I'm very thankful to report that there wasn't as much as a minor injury during that whole process. The only one that came close to an injury was the day Elder Carl Potter, bless his heart, came to the church while we were putting the new roof on and he climb up on the roof with his street shoes on. We tried to warn him that the roof was very slippery without the proper shoes, but he shrugged everybody off and came on the roof anyway. Well, he had just got up to the top of the roof when he lost his footing and slide on his backside all the way down the roof, and onto the ground he fell. I just knew he was hurt, but I guess he was too embarrassed. He got up from the ground, and without looking back or saying a word to anybody he just got in his car and left the property. We never had a minute's trouble out of him since then.

Our congregants were so excited about the new place. When we had put the trusses in place for the roof, a storm came through and blew all of them down. Some were just lying down on top of the wall, and we set them back in place. Thank God they were not damaged. We only lost about a day's work in order to reset the trusses.

Now many of you know that when God starts blessings, the devil starts messing. We were on our way to actually having a nice church to be presented to the Lord when our neighbors in the rear, a VFW, became concerned about a church being in front of them. A representative from them came over to talk with me and said they didn't want a church in front of them. I said very boldly and with excitement that it was too bad, we are doing it. They told me that we would never have a church there, and I spoke boldly, *"We will see!"*

Well, we did see. Somehow their attorney pulled some strings downtown, and less than thirty days later, we got a letter from the city telling us that if our building was not completed in thirty days, they were going to completely demolish our building, leaving us with a vacant lot. We were devastated to say the least. To keep from being stuck with the property, the owner was nice enough to let us sign the property back over to him. Hurt, injured, and remorseful, we actually found a church building that was for sale in a different location of the city. I approached the pastor, and the congregation agreed to sell us the church. They were building another church in another area of the city and wanted to move. We had already established a letter of commitment from the bank for $50,000.00, which was not near enough but was carried over from the Liberty Street project. They assured us that they would be willing to carry a second mortgage. Lord, we were beyond excitement and were giving praises to Almighty God for what he has done for us. We were going to have a permanent place of worship. *Thank God!*

The church had a nice-size sanctuary and a basement with a few classrooms. It was an ideal place for our congregation size, with some room for growth. We were so happy and satisfied because I felt like the Lord had finally put in the place where we needed to be.

Well, little did we realize the enemy never stops nor take breaks. After about six months the other church members was ready to go into their new church and feeling very comfortable about closing the very next morning.

The night before their closing the pastor called and asked if we were ready to close. I said yes and reminded him of what they said about carrying the second mortgage for us. Shockingly he said they were not interested in doing a second mortgage with us and was expecting the balance or we had to vacate immediately. *Wow! Wow!* I didn't know what to do or where to go. If something wasn't done right now, our church would have been broken up and dispersed. It was beyond me seeing that happening for we had come too far for that to happen. Without talking with my wife, I told our congregation that if we stayed together, the Lord would work miracles for us, so we started having service at our house, which wasn't even ours. We were renting it. Sunday morning and for Bible study we met in the lower part of our house. We were living in a split-level house, which work out just fine. We didn't lose a member during the transition from the church building to the house to finding another place to worship. As was in any of our lowest points or places, God has always showed up and provided better and beyond what we ever expected of him. *Thank God*!

Victory over Every Challenge

I have been pastoring now for many years, and most of those years, the mind-set of people has been about the same. The people always needed to be encouraged. I'm not sure whether it is because of the lack of praying together or individually. I know there were times when there was no Bible study since the building was in such in disarray. It seems to me that the enemy uses every opportunity to separate and divide.

I'm reminded in the scripture of Nehemiah. Nehemiah was allowed to go back to his homeland to see the devastation there. I think it was awesome for him to be able to encourage his countrymen to the point where the Scriptures says, "So built they the walls around Jerusalem for the people had a mind to work." What an awesome exclamation to be able to have such a testimony. I know that every church project has it challenges, but the Lord God has the power to see you through and to help you complete the work you've started with peace and victory. *Hallelujah*!

There were similar experiences when building the church of *Love Temple COGIC* in Winston-Salem, North Carolina, and *The Garden of Eden* in Eden, North Carolina. We were in Winston-Salem for about twenty years and we were trying to find a permanent place of worship. After many disappointments and running into dead-end situations and with every one of those places renovated and converted into churches, we finally found the property at 2946 Ivy Avenue and Thirtieth Street.

There was a small building on the property that was used as a drive-up café. I went in and converted the small area into a place to worship. It was kind off L-shaped that would house about seventy-five people. I built a small pulpit, which made the place real cozy. During the time of renovating the place, little did I realize that the electricity in the building was still on. I asked an electrician, a friend of mine at that time, to check the meter that was in the building. He had no idea and neither did I that the electricity was still on in the building until the electrician took his large screwdriver to test the wires. A large *bang* was heard, and electrical sparks flew all over the place. Well, both of us hit the ground to hide from the explosion. We simply looked at each other in a surprised fear. After that we simply laughed from what had just happened. We learned that the power had been left on the building from months earlier. *Look at God*! It was as if the Lord had already set things up for us. Not only was there electricity but the water was on as well. We had lights and had use of the bathrooms too. What a mighty God! A building permit had already been established, and we didn't have to get one because whoever owned the property before us had already paid for a building permit and also laid concrete for the footing and the first course of blocks for a restaurant, which ended up being the exact size of our church building. We continued having services in the small area, enjoying each other in worship and inviting others to come and worship with us. It took a few years to accomplish it because we were building and paying for materials as we went along in the ministry. I was doing all the labor during that time, except for one of our brothers in the church, Brother Donald Lowery, who refused anything we tried to give him. He laid all the blocks for the church and then layered all the bricks for our church, and he didn't take a dime. The most we could do for him was give him good meal from time to time. *What a blessing!* I drew the plans and built the church accordingly. I trained the men, mostly in the church, to build along with me. I had a tremendous burden in my heart for building a church for the Lord and his people. I never gave a thought about being paid a salary or getting a money at all for building the church. Many disciples were gained as we built little by little until there was a shell that started to resemble a building, let alone a church. The excitement grew as I was trying to accomplish the vision that the Lord had given me. Well, it wasn't so much about me, I don't think; but I wanted to make my pastor, Bishop Wyoming W. Wells, to be proud of me for he always wanted a church in Winston Salem. You see Bishop Wells passed away a few years before all this took place. I remember during the time of his death that I was so devastated because I wanted him to see what I had accomplished. I was praying about those very things, and it was as if the Lord spoke to me in the prayer, "The things you wanted your pastor to see, he already saw it." From that point on I was satisfied in my spirit about the ministry in Winston-Salem.

The church in Winston-Salem was built from the ground up. The greatest toll was on me since I was physically building the church in Winston-Salem and having to minister to them at the same time. I'm afraid some members of our congregation started to notice the difference in my preaching, and rather than continue to pray for the pastor, some of them began to complain. With that being said, it's difficult for me find the words to express how the pressures really took its toll on me. There were times when I entertain various thoughts. I was trying to work on a full-time job, be a husband to my wife, be a father to my children, be a pastor, and continue ministering to the people in the church and overseeing and laboring with my own hands. It was just about more than I could handle. My family tried, I believe, to support me as much as they could but had no earthly idea what to do during that time. It was as if I was all by myself, me and God, and I couldn't see from God the comfort I thought I needed.

When I looked up and saw the sanctuary enclosed and dried in, I became so overjoyed, along with my wife and children. The church members were beyond excitement, for they finally saw the church that they had tried to envision for so long. As I was traveling to various cities around Winston-Salem, I stopped by in Greensboro to finish a job that I had to do when the Lord laid on my heart to stop the Georgia Pacific paneling company in Greensboro. I went to the manufacturer and asked for the president, who just happened to be in his office. His secretary allowed me to go in and see him. He asked me to sit down and asked, "What can I do for you?" I told him that we are building a church in Winston Salem and that I needed his help. He listened as I continued to explain to him how he could help us. We needed sixty-six pieces of one-fourth inches paneling to put in our sanctuary. He thought for a minute and said to me, "It's going to take two-and-a-half SKUS of paneling. If you will pay for the half SKU, then I will give you the other two and deliver them to your church without any cost to whatsoever." I thanked him and started rejoicing before I left his office. Those are just some of the things the Lord had done to show his favor toward us. Again, we were beyond excitement just seeing our church building coming together. After installing the paneling, it was time for the ceilings to be installed. Well, the company that I worked for told me that I could have all the ceiling material to do our ceiling in our building, which included the sanctuary, the offices, the hallways, the toilets, the kitchen, and the mechanical room. Hallelujah! It had to have been a favor.

Charlie Marshall was a working friend who owned shopping centers around town and he had a brother who owned a heating and air conditioning company. He told me how impressed he was with our choir's singing and that he really loved their singing. I was telling him about our need for the mechanical work for heating and air conditioning. Well, he told me not worry about a thing. He would install all the mechanical materials and the labor was at no cost to us. It had to be the favor of God. Thank you, Jesus! Charlie Marshall sent his carpenters to help me build the choir, pulpit, and the altar areas for no charge at all. I believe the Lord has done that in part to really encourage my heart from all the weight I was under. We were able to get enough carpet and floor tile to cover the entire building. One of the greatest joys was when it was time to order the pews for the church. We didn't have enough money to pay for them. I remember so well, after talking with the company about the pews, that they told us when we got the money to pay for them, to just call them back. I was somewhat content with that and was going to try take care of some other things when my wife called and told me, "Guess what?" Of course I had no idea, but she said the company called about the pews and told us that they are ready and wanted to deliver them the next week. They also said that we could make installments until they are paid off. *What an awesome God we serve!* Well, things continue to fall in place for because of his favor. There was some finish work that had to be done, but because we were limited with funds, we would have to wait or the Lord would have to favor us, and He did.

I was riding in the neighborhood of our church where there were warehouses and noticed a lumber company in one of them Well, I stop and looked around, and this place had all the lumber we needed to finish the inside of the church. I was so amazed that such a small place could have so much in it. After looking around, the salesman came up to me ask if I was looking for something in particular. I told that I needed much of if he had on display. Oh man! He told me that I could get any and all I needed to do the work at the church and that he would deliver it for me. Of course, he said I could pay back on time. Wow! He did it again!

We got all the materials we needed and paid for on time. Thank God! Not too long after that I drove around to the warehouse again looking for the lumber company and there no sign of them. It was as if they were never there. I knew from that the Lord had given us favor once again. I asked other businesses in the area about that particular lumber company and they that they have never heard of nor seen anything like a lumber company in this warehouse. My God, what a miracle! Hallelujah!

Another joy of ours was when the pews were delivered and men began putting the pews together. They had working system that simply blew our minds. To watch them assemble the pews and began putting them in place in the sanctuary was almost more than we could bear. After they had place all the pews in place and made them permanent, we were like children going in and out of each pew until we went through all of them, including the pulpit and the choir. We were more than ecstatic when we were able to have our first service in our new church. We exalted and praise God that day like never before. It was also during that time that we were asked to have a radio broadcast. We accepted the challenge and began broadcasting every Sunday afternoon at 4:00 p.m. It seems the entire city would tune in because Love Temple had one the baddest choirs in the area. The Love Temple Victory Choir was well-known all over the eastern part of this country. My wife in many ways was the psalmist, son George was on the organ, son Scott was on the drums, Sonji was one of the choir directors, and Jerri helped carry the sopranos on the choir. Our son Jeffrey became the first preacher among the children, and George II and Sonji soon followed. *All honor and glory certainly belongs to the Lord!*

There were two churches of God in Christ in the Winston-Salem area at that time that were trying to move from missions to church building. The struggle was severe in that only a few people were able to see and understand the vision. After many moves and failures to be established, God seemed to start turning things in favor of the vision He gave. The scriptures were being fulfilled when God said it and now He was doing it.

The other church of God in Christ was Faith Chapel. Elder John McClurkin was their pastor, and the Lord was blessing them also.

The Garden of Eden COGIC in Eden was a permanent place but was very small, and the building of about seventy-five was falling apart. It never entered my mind to benefit monetarily from either of the churches in Winston-Salem, North Carolina, or Eden, North Carolina. I just wanted to build the Lord a place of worship for the people.

The church in Eden was already built, and we made it bigger—that is, building a larger building over the small building and tearing out the small one. We did leave the floor from the existing building and tied the new into the old. It was a work of precise planning to make a new building to fit perfectly into the old floor plan, which included basement areas. Needless to say, it was quite a challenge from the start.

Little did we know that the city manager of the city of Eden was trying to block and condemn the existing building. He sent a letter to the church and to the city officials saying that the church building could not be added on to the existing property and in fact the existing building was a foot over the allotted line that was allowed for the church. In order to make changes and proceed with building, we had to appear before the Board of Variance of the city of Eden and plead our case for what we intended to do. Being a job estimator for a small construction company, I already had experience in drafting plans. I was responsible for reading and taking off plans for public and secret biddings for different projects during my building and renovation career. I drew up the plans of the projected church building along with parking.

The night that we were to appear before the Board of Variance, I took ten to twelve copies of the plans with me for the board to follow along as I explained to them our projected plans. A good representation of our church membership went along with me for support. After the meeting started, the chairman of the Board of Variance called out for our church and I went up to the designated area along with the city manager. The city manager proceeded to tell the board why he turned down our application for permit to build the church on the property. He said to the board that our existing building was a foot over the allotted place at the property line, which meant that the existing building was against the city code and should have never been built to begin with. I had no idea that the city manager had already sent out letters telling the city officials what his plans were. Well, when it was my turn to speak, you've heard in the scriptures when it says, and I'm paraphrasing now, take no thoughts in what you should say or do but in the very hour the Holy Spirit will give you what to say. I addressed the board, and I don't remember all that I said to them, but they listened attentively. And when I finished, the city manager came back with more condemning information. When he finished, I came back with a rebuttal, explaining the plans for the new church, and told them that as long as the church is in existence it should be considered a historical place for the city of Eden, North Carolina.

Well, after about forty-five minutes of deliberation and questions from the Board of Variance, the chairman of the committee members asked about the parking around the church. When there's a new building erected in the city, there had to be enough of street parking to accommodate the people in the church. I believe it has to be a parking space for every four persons.

The chairman of the committee said to me, "Reverend, if everybody went to church on Sunday, there wouldn't be a parking problem anyway, would it?"

I answered him, "No, sir."

His response after that was, *"Reverend, I move that you go and build your church."* The rest of members on the board unanimously said *"Amen."* We received an applause from the audience that were in the room. I didn't realize how stressful that meeting was on me until we got outside of the building and all my strength left me and I fell to the ground. Some of the young men who were there picked me up and helped me to my car. God had already began to give the church favor. *Hallelujah!*

The next day we paid for our building permit to begin building the new church. I'm convinced that "if God be for you, He is more than the world is against you." *Praise the Lord*!

When laying out the church, there had to be great pride and care so that the floor of the new building would be exactly the same height as the existing floor of the old building. The measurements had to be exact, or the building project would be a failure. There was partial basement of the existing building that had to tie right into the new one. Precision is what it took for everything to come together. I'm very proud to say that it did. *Praise the Lord*! We laid the footing for the new building, and the building was on its way. We poured the footing and began laying the bricks for the church. The church members were so excited and not only them but the entire community was excited for us. As we were having the church bricked, we installed the windows and the glass front, which gave the building sophistication to say the least. The roof was erected, and the electrician began the rough in for the electrical work. There was an older man who showed up from what seemed like nowhere and joined the church. Well, he worked profusely throughout the day and early evening until we had the old building torn completely out. After cleaning up all the debris from the old building, it was time to start on the interior of the new building.

After building over the existing building, we began tying everything to fit. We covered the floor with new carpet. From the foundation to the electrical, both rough and finish work, to the walls, the exterior and the inner, were brick, to the plumbing, both rough and finish. The ceilings were a two-by-two gypsum panel for sound control.

The church, when finished, seated around 350 people, which did not include the choir and pulpit areas.

It was in my heart to prepare all our parishioners for the building experience as the Lord was directing us to fast, pray, and continue the Bible study, which would prevent the enemy from entering into our midst and cause division and dissension. The church did very good for a while, but as time went on, the pressure started to take its toll on me from the labor and some of our members began to feel restless and, not to mention, having trouble continuing the service while the building was going up around them. It was taking a tremendous toll on me, for I was doing a great portion of the labor myself and trying to minister to them at the same time. I was not as focused as I should have been with all the activity that was going on. I began to be tempted and failed in some areas, but *I thank God for his mercy*! The majority of our members continued to be faithful and were excited to see all that the Lord was doing for us. As promised, the church progressed physically and in membership.

The stress level was very high as I drew the plans for both churches and was having them approved. Much of the building was done hands-on by me. I really didn't realize just how much stress was being put on me, but *to God be the glory*, the church was finished. I understand now how things were in the days of Nehemiah when he was building the walls around Jerusalem. The difference in many cases is "for the people had a mind to work." And as for me, I can say as Nehemiah said, "I'm doing a great work, and I can't come down."

There were many days of trouble and temptation, some victories and some defeats, because it took awhile to finish building the church in Eden, to see how the Lord gave the vision to build right over the old building and eventually remove the old building. After the old building was removed and seeing the new building open up into such a large area was simply mind-boggling. The inside walls of the sanctuary was brick. The same as the outside. I began framing the walls that separated the foyer from the sanctuary. I also framed the walls for women and men's toilets. Walls were built that would separate the stalls in each toilet. I installed paneling over the frame work both in the back of the church and around the choir area. We used the existing pulpit area but made it larger. The ceilings were of a two-by-two lay-in pattern with acoustical effects for sound. Our members were so excited to see the progress made in coming to completion soon. It was very strange at first when making the transition from the small area into the large area. Most everything has changed and cost more than what the expenses were before. *But God helped us to adjust!*

We called for new pews to be installed that would match the old pews, which was a perfect match. Our first service in the new church was beyond our excitement. We hardly knew what to do with ourselves but praise God for all his blessings. *Thanks be to God* for the victory. In both churches in Winston-Salem, North Carolina, and in Eden, North Carolina, I can say, "*We did finish! Thank God!*"

Through all the trials that came to the various ministries, as well as you individually, "*God is faithful who has promised.*"

My admonition to you is to have a *heart of penitence toward God* and continue toward the mark that has been set before you. *God bless* each and every one of you!

After leaving the basement, we (Jan and myself) found a two-story house with a small commercial building attached to it. Well, I saw a chapel there that we could use in the small building for services until the chapel was completed. I made arrangements to purchase the house, building, and the land on Liberty Street and began to remove the second story from the house to convert it into a chapel. I didn't know at the time that it wasn't the Lord's will that I build a chapel there, but I was gung-ho on starting and completing the task that was ahead of us. I wish I could put it into words the pressure that was on me to present to the Lord a place to worship. I just don't know any words that could reveal to you what I believe God had put in me.

The house was not only two stories but had a large brick chimney in the center of it. With all of that, I could see the church sitting there finished. I drew up a simple plan to keep my focus on the demolition and began tearing off the existing roof, cut that second story off the house, tore the chimney completely out, and gutted the entire house to make ready for building a church in place of the house, not a single-dwelling house but a house of God! That was a tremendous victory for me just to see that much done in a short period of time. *All praises to the Lord!*

By the way, the men who had joined the church were the ones who assisted in the work. Some of them had jobs during the day and would come when they got off work. Others that worked at night would lie down for a while when they got off and then come to do whatever was needed of them. They made me even more excited because of their excitement in the project. There were a few who had gained employment to what was needed.

I prepared the walls for trussers, and when they were delivered, we set each one of them by hand and started placing the plywood. Well, before we could complete that part of the roof, a big storm came through the city and blew each of the trussers down. Someone passing by the church saw what had happened and called me and told me that the roof had fallen down. I was so broken and outdone, but I somehow mustered up enough strength to salvage each one of them and build it back.

Being so excited about everything going on, little did I know that the devil was not going to allow a church to be built on that property. There was a VFW center in the back of our building, and their attorney approached to complain about our church going up in front of them and told me that "a church will never be in the spot where we are."

I told him with a lot of confidence that the property was ours and that there was going to be a church right there. He said, "We'll see then." And I said, "We'll see then." I was so proud of myself for standing up to the attorney until about two weeks later I received a letter from the city stating that the building had to be finished in thirty days or else they are going to come in and tear everything down. Wow! Talk about a blow to my ego and everything else I believed in. There was no way we could complete and finish the church in thirty days.

I had already received a letter of commitment from First Federal Bank downtown Winston-Salem, which is another story of its own. Anyway, I went back to the people who we were buying the property from and explained to them the situation, *and they allowed us to sign the property back over to them*! *My, my, my, my, what a miracle*!

Well, there was a church building near the boy's club off Stadium Drive that was for sale, and after talking with the pastor of the church, he said they would accept the letter of commitment and possibly do a second mortgage on the church for us. We moved right in, thinking and thanking the Lord for what he had done on our behalf. It was a white congregation moving into another area of the city, and we thought for certain that it was a sure thing for our church. After ninety days, when the congregation was supposed to take the second mortgage out to purchase the church, the night before signing, the pastor of the church called and asked if we had the money for the second mortgage and said that they would not be signing and told us that we needed to vacate the church and property. I was devastated but didn't want to show my emotions or weaknesses to our congregation. I said we would have services in lower part of our house. I never thought to discuss it with my wife, but she went right along with it. She had to have been feeling the same as me, with us not even talking about it until later on. We stayed at our house for a few weeks until I'm not sure if it was Jan or me saw some property up on the corner of Ivy and Thirtieth Street. It was a corner lot that had a small building on it that would seat maybe fifty to seventy-five people when fixed up. Somebody said that an old man had a little cafe there with the intention of building it bigger, for there was a layout there with a footing all the way around the small building. I was told he died before he could do anything with it. When I saw it, I began to see a church building finished and the congregation just rejoicing in it. I went to the owner, and he worked out a deal with me. I signed the papers and went and told my wife. We shared it with our members. We were so excited about what the Lord had done.

I began renovating the small building, preparing it for service. Well, we all got together and started working. I didn't know if we could have the electrical service installed, so I asked an electrician friend of mine at the time if he would come and check out the service for us. He met me there, and he started looking at the places where the meter was. While checking, a big spark of electricity jump out of the box and we found out that the electricity was already there. *Wow! Another miracle!* For it had been a few years since the man that owned the property had died and yet the service was still on. *To God be the glory!*

We managed to get the small building ready for service, and when finished, it was kind of L-shape and we were sitting on top of each other. But the closeness made it very comfortable for worship.

All along my preaching was inspirational and people were accepting the Lord as their savior and joining the church.

There were many days of trouble and temptation, some victories and some defeats because it took awhile to finish building the church in Winston-Salem than in Eden. *But thanks be to God* for the victory, both in Winston-Salem, North Carolina, and in Eden, North Carolina.

Through all the trials that came to the various ministries as well as individually, God remained faithful to his promise.

My admonition to you is to have a *heart of penitence* and *continue* toward the mark that has been set before you. God bless each and every one of you!

From the COGIC to the AME Churches

In 1998 I transferred to the AME church and started attending Turners Chapel AME church in High Point, North Carolina. The Presiding Elder Benjamin Foust presented me and I was accepted in the Western District Conference that year, and the church accepted my credentials. Attending the church every Sunday and Bible study on Wednesday nights prepared me for our annual conference that was held in various parts of the Western North Carolina Conference of the Second District of the African Methodist Episcopal Church. I was presented to the annual conference that year and was told by Bishop Vinton Anderson that to be ordained I had to go to the Board of Examiners for two years.

After two years the Western North Carolina Annual conference ordained me and assigned me to my first pastorate at Joseph Temple AME Church in Laurinburg, North Carolina. I traveled back and forth to Joseph Temple AME Church for six months before the Presiding Elder of the Western District of the Western NC Conference called me and told me to get my robes for he was moving me to Pearson Memorial AME Church in High Point, North Carolina. Presiding Elder Benjamin Foust told me that he needed to get me out of the Eastern District. Thank God!

Over the years I have served approximately five churches in the Western North Carolina Conference. I have already mentioned Joseph Temple AME Church in Lauringburg, North Carolina, and Pearson Memorial AME Church in High Point, North Carolina. Pearson Memorial AME Church was nearer our home and only took approximately twenty minutes to get there. The membership was very willing to receive me and my wife as a ministerial couple. We were able to accomplish many good things both physically and spiritually. The other churches are Poplar Grove AME Church in Greensboro, North Carolina. It was much closer to our home, and we were able to establish a good working relationship with each other. The Lord added to the membership, and the church was becoming stronger and stronger. The youth department grew until we established a praise dance group under the direction of Ms. Tara Donnell and Ms. Marlene Lash. They were also working with our YPDers, which is the youth department in the AME churches. These young people were so dedicated until the dance team grew to about twenty-three to twenty-five dancers. The men were so excited about the church until I started talking about building a new church. They became the more excited. And with that excitement, the church began growing spiritually and numerically. After four and a half years, as with the AME Church, the Annual Conference sent us to St. Mathews in Burlington, North Carolina. St. Mathews AME Church in Burlington, North Carolina, had quite a challenge with a mortgage, which was very high. With God's help and the wisdom of the membership, we were able to take care of that mortgage from month to month until we were able to refinance and make the payments more affordable. After three years the Conference sent us—that is, my wife and me—to St. John AME Church in Gibsonville, North Carolina, and now St. John AME in Gibsonville, North Carolina. We were able to stay longer there than any other churches. St John is a family church that works closely together. I was able to build a new pastor's office from what was an area used for storage, and I must say it turned out better than what some expected. With the help of some of the men, we were able to get it done. A very proud moment! We were able also to make repairs on the church to beautify the building. I was able to encourage the church to raise funds to replace a furnace that had gone bad and to install a new roof. *Thank God!* As it is perhaps in churches across the board, we have gained members and have also lost members through death and with some just leaving. It seemed to have caused our membership to grow closer together. We had many challenges but also many victories. After six years the Lord has been mighty, mighty good to the church and to me as well. *All glory belongs to the Lord!*

It really seems to me now that I was chosen to be a troubleshooter for each of these churches. I'm very proud to say that each of the churches in which I pastored have done better than they had done before. *Thanks be to God!* This is my last year as a pastor in the AME Church. The 2018–2019 annual conference is my last year in pastoral service. It has been my complete honor to serve in the capacity of pastor for these many years and pray that my service has been uplifting and beneficial to the African Methodist Episcopal Church of the Second District and have brought glory and honor to the name of God our Father and our Lord and Savior Jesus, the Christ.

I have no idea what the next chapters are for me in this grand old church. I am willing, able, and ready to see what the end is going to be. With God's help I know everything is going to be all right. Throughout my life in ministry, the Lord's will and purpose has always been revealed. I have no doubt that his purpose will continue to be manifested, not only for me but to all who continues in his will.

The Next Chapter

The next chapter of my life would ordinarily be blank. In the AME Church, when you reach the age of seventy-five, they retire you, which means you superannuate. Generally, if you have a home church, you can return to it; and under the leadership of the present pastor, if he wants to, he would allow you to take part in the services. If the Presiding Elder calls you, you might get a chance to preach in another church in the district. If not that, you can return to the annual conference and answer the roll call at the opening of the conference.

Upon retirement you don't have another church to pastor, you don't have a congregation that would call on you, your pastor friends may or may not call on you to preach for them. It's as if after you have spent all those years in ministry, there you are by yourself and all alone.

Where are the congregants that you bonded with, those who told you ever so often how much they love you? The realization has taken its stand in your life: that you are by yourself and have no ministry, no church, and no congregation to go to. Your family is there to give you as much support as they can. Your wife would like to console you, but she is struggling with some of the same things. Maybe sleepless nights and lonely days. These are the ordinary thing you have to deal with.

But God wouldn't bring you this far to leave you. Our God always has a plan and a purpose for you, especially when you have been faithful to his call on life. I know the enemy wants you to get lost in your present situation, to think and feel like you've spent all this time in the ministry and these are the results. *The devil is a liar!*

"*Thanks be to God who giveth us the victory through Christ Jesus our savior.*"

"I'm convinced that death nor life shall be able to separate me from the love of God."

My God is the controller of all life has to offer, and as Jeremiah 29:11 says, the blessings of the Lord be upon all "for I know the thoughts that I think toward you, saith the Lord, thoughts of peace, and not of evil, to give you an expected end."

This chapter and all other chapters of your life are in the hands of the Almighty God.

The blessings of the Lord be upon all of you who reads this book!

Printed in August 2022
by Arrowhead Graphics Inc. - USA